RALLY

Janice K. Taylor

Illustrated by Savannah Horton

Rally by Janice K. Taylor

Copyright © 2021, 2024. All rights reserved.

ALL RIGHTS RESERVED: No part of this book may be reproduced, stored, or transmitted, in any form, without the express and prior permission in writing of the author. This book may not be circulated in any form of binding or cover other than that in which it is currently published.

This book is licensed for your personal enjoyment only. All rights are reserved. The author does not grant you rights to resell or distribute this book without prior written consent of author/copyright owner of this book. This book must not be copied, transferred, sold or distributed in any way.

Disclaimer: The Author will not be held responsible for repercussions to anyone who utilizes the subject of this book for illegal, immoral or unethical use.

This book or part thereof may not be reproduced in any form, stored in a retrieval system, or transmitted in any form by any means-electronic, mechanical, photocopy, recording or otherwise-without prior written consent of the publisher, except as provided by United States of America copyright law.

ISBN: 978-1-958792-10-0

Illustrated by Savannah Horton

Dedication

To Angie and her family who helped save Rally and to all the people who work every day to rescue animals in need.

"Mrs. Holland, Mrs. Holland!"

I was outside watering my flowers when I heard the shouts coming from the road. It was a bright and sunny June day and that made it difficult to see who was calling my name.

I held my hand over my eyes to block the sun as I looked toward the road. In the distance, I saw two figures running my way. As they came closer, I recognized Josh and Alan, two teen boys that live close by.

As they approached, I saw a scared look on their faces. "What is it, guys?" I asked.

"We were in the woods down there," Josh pointed to the small wooded area down the road from where I live. It was a favorite place for people in the neighborhood to take a walk in nature.

"We saw this little puppy lying by a tree," Josh said.

"Yeah, it was all dirty and grungy looking," Alan panted, out of breath from running.

"Not sure if it was dead, but it didn't look too good."

Being the animal lover that I am, and having an especially soft heart for dogs, I had to go see.

"Show me where it is," I said as I hopped on my golf cart that I use to drive around our lake area. I motioned to the boys, "Jump on and let's go."

Josh and Alan jumped on the golf cart and they directed me to the dog.

There, in a patch of grass by a tree, was a small, dark, reddish-colored dog with matted fur.

As we approached, it did not try to get up. I could tell it was very weak. I assumed it had been abandoned or was lost and had been living in the woods for a while.

I talked to the puppy. It lifted its head to look at me, but did not try to stand.

It was alive, but barely!

"Guys, help me lift it onto the cart and we'll take it to my house," I said.

We carefully lifted the dog onto the floor of the golf cart and hurried back to my place.

"It looks like it's covered in fleas and its fur is all matted," I commented.

I went to my garage and found a tub to use to bathe the little male puppy. I found some flea shampoo that I kept on-hand for our dogs, so we used lots of it to wash him.

It was amazing! He looked like a different dog! The dirty, dark-reddish colored dog was now white and fluffy. The bath water was full of dead fleas when we finished.

We gave him some food and water and he seemed to perk up.

"Hey, Buddy, how are you doing? You're a really pretty dog now," I told him.

I talked to him and petted him, but he still didn't have a lot of energy. He spent the rest of the day just lying around.

That night, I made a bed for him with a really soft blanket so he would feel comfortable.

I placed the bed in my bedroom and he slept there all night.

The next morning he ate well, but still did not have a lot of energy. I tried to stand him up, but he did not have the energy to stand on his own.

"This little guy needs some medical help," I told my husband, Kevin.

He agreed.

I telephoned the vet that takes care of our dogs. He said to bring him to his office and he would examine him to see what was wrong.

The vet gave him a thorough exam.

"This dog is very sick," the vet told us. "He has lost a lot of blood because of all the flea bites. He will need a blood transfusion or he will likely die."

I felt so sorry for this poor little puppy, and I wanted him to have a chance to live.

I told Dr. Williams, "Do whatever you need to do to save him."

"I will do all I can," he said, "I think he's been on his own in that woods for quite a while. He's lucky he was found. I don't think he would have lived much longer in his condition."

I gave Buddy, (that's the name we're calling him), a pat on the head and said, "You're going to be ok, Buddy. Dr. Williams will take good care of you."

Dr. Williams has been a very good vet to our dogs and I had faith that he could help Buddy.

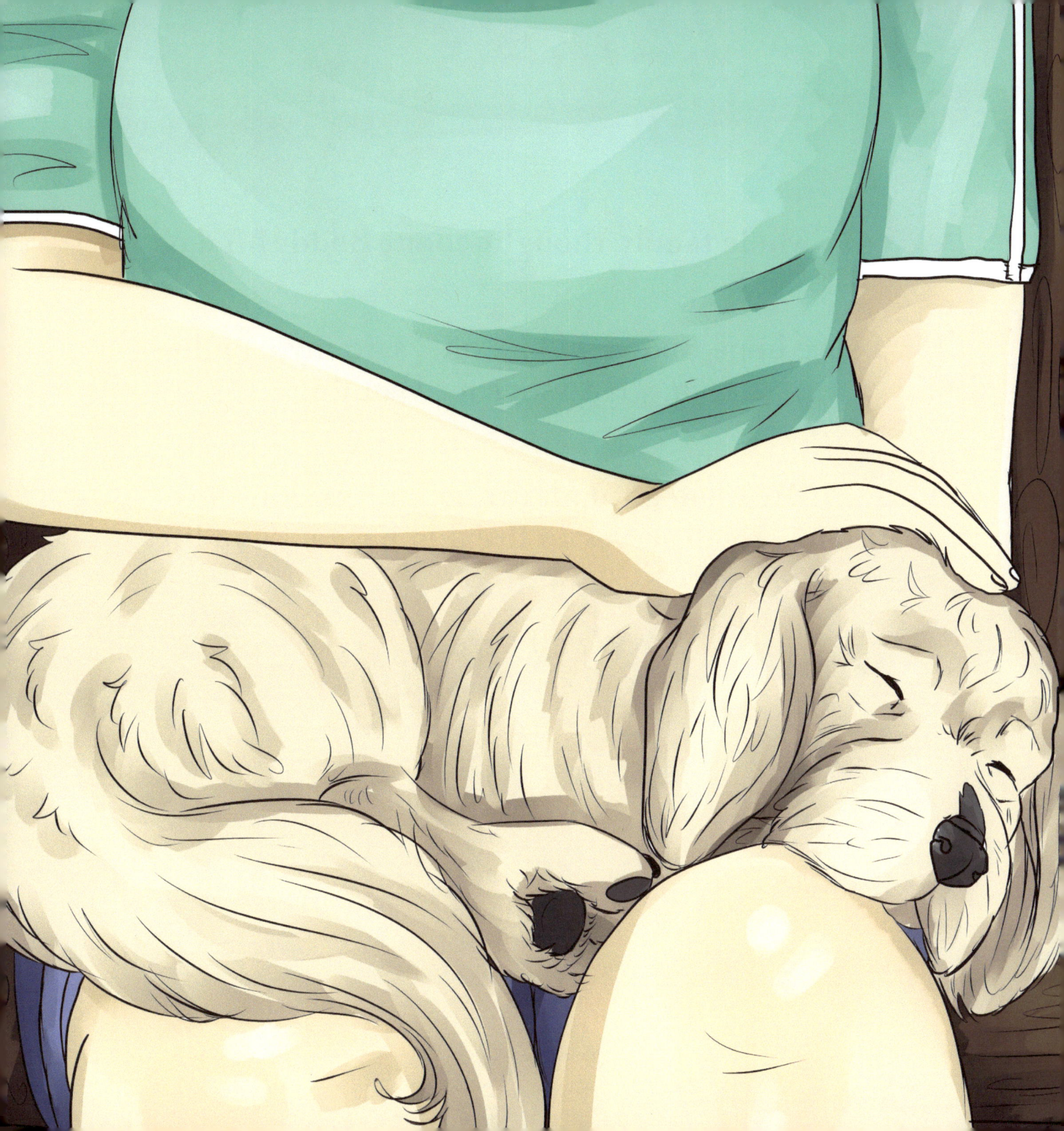

My whole family thought about Buddy all day.

"I sure hope Buddy will be ok," said my daughter, Karen. "He's such a sweet dog."

"He's had a tough life so far," said my son Ethan. "He deserves to live and have a good life."

We all agreed.

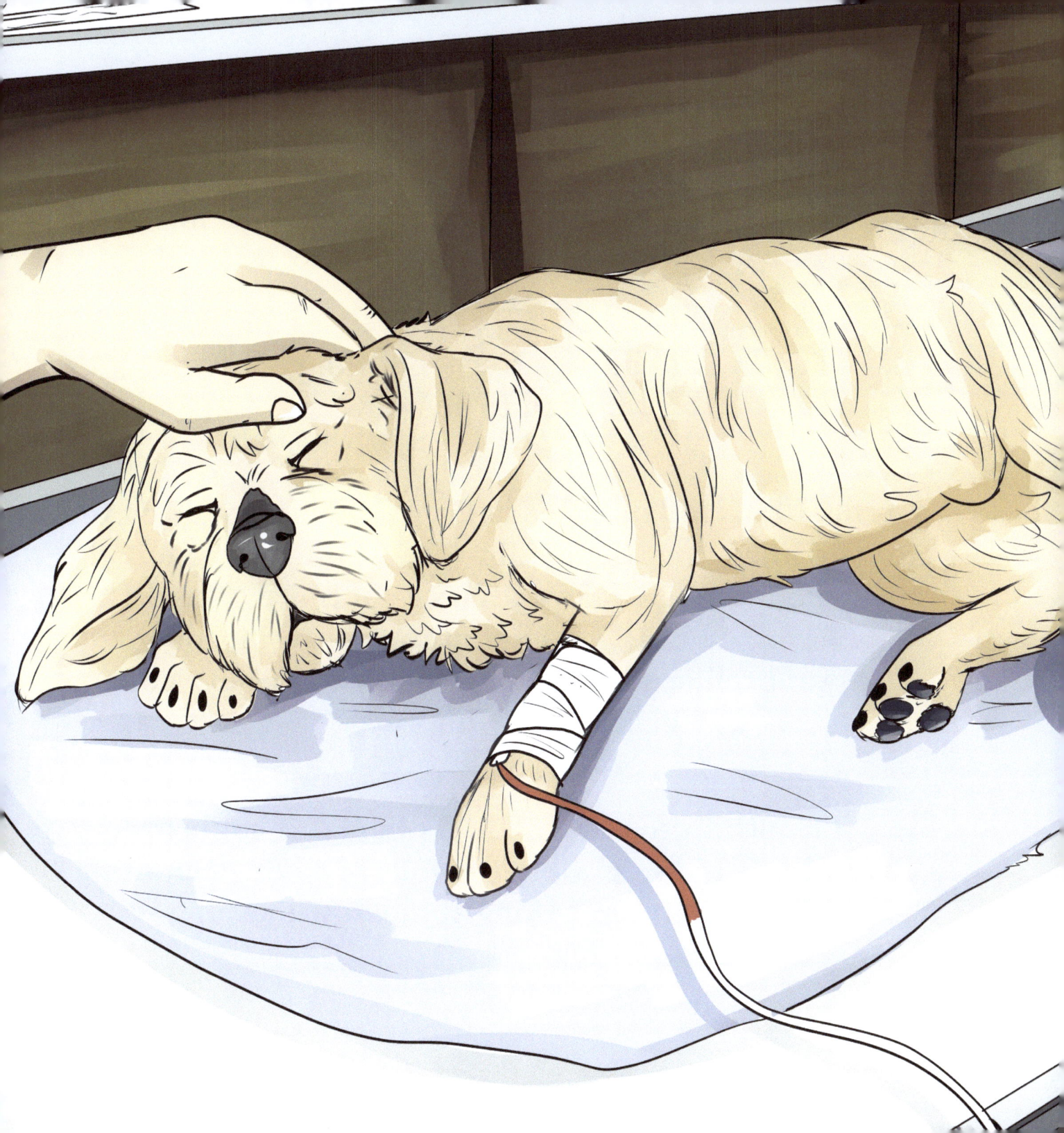

The next day, we were so nervous waiting for Dr. Williams to call with news about Buddy. We tried to go about our lives, but it was difficult to concentrate on anything else besides Buddy.

Finally, late in the afternoon, the phone rang. I rushed to answer.

"Hello, Mrs. Holland, this is Dr. Williams. I wanted to let you know that Buddy did very well with the blood transfusion. He is awake and has a lot more energy than before. You can pick him up tomorrow morning. I want to keep him one more day to be sure he continues to improve."

"Thank you so much, Dr. Williams. That is great news! We are so grateful to you for saving Buddy. We'll be there first thing tomorrow morning."

When I told my family the news, we all gave a big shout, HURRAY! We slept well that night knowing Buddy was going to be fine.

The next morning, we were up early and ready to pick up Buddy. When we walked in Dr. Williams's office, we couldn't believe our eyes!

"Is this Buddy?" I asked, hardly recognizing this energetic little dog that was walking around his office.

"He has really come alive since he had the blood transfusion," said Dr. Williams. "We also bathed him again and gave him some medicine for the flea bites and infection. He's going to be fine now."

We were so excited and thankful that Buddy was ok. We gave Dr. Williams a big thank you and took Buddy home with us.

When we arrived home, Buddy was a ball of energy, running around the yard and playing with our two dogs.

That evening, our family was eating dinner and Buddy was curled up under the table at my feet. We talked about what a big difference there was in Buddy and what a sweet, lovable puppy he is.

"I think we should change his name to Rally," I suggested, "because he rallied so much from a dog that was nearly dead to a lively ball of energy."

We all agreed that Rally would be a great name for him; so Rally it was. For the next few days, Rally continued to become stronger and healthier.

"I know we all love Rally," I said to my family one evening, "but the fact is we really can't keep him. We already have two dogs."

"We need to find just the right family for him. He deserves a family that will give him lots of love and attention," said Karen.

"We all agree to that," I replied. "Rally has had a tough start in life and he deserves a very loving family for his forever home."

The next day, I started asking around and also posted the story of Rally on Facebook.

In fact, I started a Facebook page for Rally with pictures of him when we first found him and several pictures of him now. The page was called "Rallying for Rally".

One evening, our phone rang and I answered.

"Hello, my name is Alice Carson. I saw the information about Rally on the Facebook page.

My husband and I used to have a dog that looked very much like Rally. He grew old and died a few years ago. Although we wanted to get another dog after that, we just never did. When we saw Rally, we thought he could be just the dog for us."

Mrs. Carson had a kind voice and after hearing her story, I had a feeling they could be a good family for Rally. I gave Mrs. Carson our address and told her to come tomorrow at 1:00.

The next day at 1:00, Mr. and Mrs. Carson arrived. "Welcome to our home," I said. "Come in and meet Rally."

Rally took right to them. They petted him and threw his ball for him. He licked them and wagged his tail. He seemed very happy with the Carsons.

"We have missed our dog very much and would love to make our home Rally's forever home," said Mr. Carson.

"We are both retired now and we are home most of the time. We would be there to give him the love and attention he deserves. We have a big, fenced backyard where he can run and play," Mrs. Carson added.

We were all so very happy to see how well Rally took to the Carsons. We knew this was going to work out great for everyone, especially for Rally.

The Carsons continued to post pictures of Rally on the Facebook page I created for him.

We could tell Rally was in a loving home and was very happy. We were delighted with his progress.

I will always remember that day in June when I first saw that very sick, helpless puppy lying limp on the grass in the woods.

I am so thankful to Josh and Alan for finding him and letting me know, so we could all work together to help him become a healthy, happy puppy and live a loving life that he deserves (as all dogs do).

The End

Author Janice K. Taylor lives in Columbus, Indiana, with her husband and their toy poodle, Bailey.

Janice is a graduate of Indiana University, where she obtained her degrees in Elementary Education and Library Science. She taught for many years in Columbus and was also an elementary librarian for several years. She is currently retired and enjoys traveling, boating, clogging, knitting, walks with Bailey and, of course, reading and writing.

www.ingramcontent.com/pod-product-compliance
Lightning Source LLC
LaVergne TN
LVHW072114070426
835510LV00002B/51

9 781958 792100